No Sign

PHOENIX POETS

PETER BALAKIAN

No Sign

THE UNIVERSITY OF CHICAGO PRESS

Chicago and London

The University of Chicago Press, Chicago 60637
The University of Chicago Press, Ltd., London
© 2022 by The University of Chicago

Published 2022
Printed in the United States of America

31 30 29 28 27 26 25 24 23 22   1 2 3 4 5

ISBN-13: 978-0-226-78407-6 (cloth)
ISBN-13: 978-0-226-78410-6 (e-book)
DOI: https://doi.org/10.7208/chicago/9780226784106.001.0001

Library of Congress Cataloging-in-Publication Data

Names: Balakian, Peter, 1951- author.
Title: No sign / Peter Balakian.
Other titles: Phoenix poets.
Description: Chicago ; London : The University of Chicago Press, 2022. |
    Series: Phoenix poets
Identifiers: LCCN 2021032855 | ISBN 9780226784076 (cloth) | ISBN
    9780226784106 (ebook)
Subjects: LCGFT: Poetry.
Classification: LCC PS3552.A443 N6 2022 | DDC 811/.54—dc23
LC record available at https://lccn.loc.gov/2021032855

♾ This paper meets the requirements of ANSI/NISO Z39.48-1992
(Permanence of Paper).

to my sisters and brother,
PAM, JIM, *and* JAN

CONTENTS

ACKNOWLEDGMENTS

The author thanks the editors of the following publications where these poems first appeared:

AGNI: "Walking the Ruined City"
Atlantic: "Pomegranate"
Consequence: "Yellow Lilies," "Outside Arshile Gorky's Studio"
Green Mountains Review: "History, Bitterness"
Harvard Review: "Tung Lai Shun"
Literary Imagination: "Revenant Love," "Matza," "Fig"
New Letters: "Okra"
New Yorker: "Eggplant," "Zucchini"
Paris Review: "Shadow Grid"
Ploughshares: "Stalled in Traffic"
Plume: "Leaving the Big City"
Poem-a-Day: "Ode to the Douduk," "Waiting for a Number"
Poetry: "Head of Anahit/British Museum"
Prairie Schooner: "Summer Ode," "Walnut," "Grape Leaves"
Progressive: "Tomatoes"
Tikkun: "Coming to Istanbul"
Yale Review: "How Much I Love You," "Bulgur"

The poem "No Sign" in a slightly earlier version was published in a limited edition in 2020 by Arrowsmith Press (Cambridge, MA).

With thanks for conversations: Askold, Bruce, Karen, Mary, Rachel, Robert Jay, and Sven.

One

HISTORY, BITTERNESS

A phone booth August/ Yaddo/ Saratoga Springs—air
of the Tiffany parlor—sour scent of empty wine bottles,

my friend handed me the sweating receiver: "Go ahead—say hello."
What could I say to James Baldwin who was dying in the south of France?

No name in the street. Paris. Algiers. Little Rock, you can fill it in . . .
I'm sitting at Les Deux Magots with my NY Yankees umbrella in my lap,

a wide glass of wine from some vineyard of Burgundy in my hand,
recalling that Baldwin sat here drinking scotch all day and writing

as friends dropped by. And it hits me: just over Pont de Sully my great uncle
sat in a big treaty room in 1919 representing Armenia (did it exist?) in a fancy

hotel with others who hoped for a nation in return for the slaughter.
Baldwin knew Sartre and de Beauvoir, he saw Camus pass by.

It was 1958 and the Algerian cabby who dropped him off drunk
on the curb was half-blind from the revolution.

Bang bang bang goes the heart. Mr. Baldwin was dying in a sensual village
in the south of France. After a week at Versailles my uncle came to that hotel room

where in the closet of his head a big white sheet floated over the Black Sea.
What did rape and massacre mean? Fail-proof, shattered, bitten-off

words that floated over the bridge into the carnival horns of night.
A few months earlier Miles Davis passed Baldwin at Les Deux Magots

on his way to play for Louis Malle's *Ascenseur pour l'échafaud*
the spurting air of love love love slipping from the valves—

the spit and breath of night in Paris off the torpid brown
Seine where Paul Celan had disappeared not long before.

Hiss hiss hiss goes the heart. It's 1958 and Camus still walks
the boulevard—the war in Algeria is daily acid in the river.

What are degrees of separation? Private myths? Illusions?
My aunt the surrealist might call them chance meetings.

Do we invent proximities for our need, for salvation, for love?
Wilson, Clemenceau, Lloyd George, names my uncle scrawled

on a map of the dispossessed—on a wall in a hotel of cards
where Dixieland horns played at a banquet for the Grande Armée

and the next map of Europe was shuffled with an ace in the hole.
Miles Davis spent seven hours with Louis Malle making some

languid, piercing, hollow sliding sounds in the indeterminate dank night;
no name on the street stalked him. A few years later Baldwin moved just miles

from where my father was born in Istanbul—a few years after the Armenians
were expunged from Turkey and my grandparents left the ghost map

on the wall. It was 1919 and the flu blew along Saint-Germain where
my grandparents met my uncle that fall. I knew Baldwin's heart went hollow,

languid, and sizzled with the need to get out of America; it even led him to
the place my grandparents fled—before they landed a couple miles from Baldwin's
apartment in Harlem.

Are these degrees of separation? Or just my way of thinking about that strange
moment in a phone booth at an artists' colony in the summer of '86?

My friend said: "If you love Jimmy's work, I know he'd love to hear
from you. All good news means a lot, especially at the end."

What could I say to Mr. Baldwin? He'd helped me understand the bitter
history that had trapped me—that was trapped in me.

Istanbul, New York, Paris. No name. No street.
I was sweating into the phone. Mr. Baldwin's voice was frail but unmistakable.

TUNG LAI SHUN

In real life we don't feel—on cue—like James Dean
in *East of Eden*, shaking in a dark hallway lit by ghosts,

what is sense memory—but some jolts along the mossy fibers and dendrites
of the hippocampus—and even so, surely even the brain is bewildered.

We know that time isn't a circular abstraction we move
along with the hope of eternal return. We know that motion

and emotion are embedded in each other, and that's why

I remember how we left our coaching jackets and the prep-school boys
jogging off the field—as we disappeared into the motion

of the GW—the suspension swaying was civilization fending off Thanatos
with burning rubber and a sliding tractor trailer we whizzed by

to get to Canal Street where strings of flags lit up Mott and Pell.

Maybe there really was "no one to drive the car"
as the platters came, glistening purple, chili red,

illuminated mud wash with scallions over fish heads,
black skins of fungus, the shellac

of hacked duck rolled with green stalks in crepes,
and maybe the motion was neurochemical even if those words

weren't part of the lingo yet. Dickinson was able to
cue up emotion in a phrase that came the way

those Chinese lanterns spun our heads.
We licked the Grecian urn of chili paste.

We didn't know we were young;
time-sense was Hegel's idea but it was too far from

the senses to lick up the sweet brown hoisin that pasted our lips.

Delmore Schwartz was a fleshy ghost because he discovered
the time-sense of moving image frames that haunted his future

and helped us find the barges on the river that were unloaded on
the avenue bearing the initial of Christ into the New World,

which turned out to be an alley off Atlantic Ave. where some Syrian grocers
knew my grandmother and your grandfather.

The ice floes under the GW were piled and shanked;
white on white was Melville and original sin.

We loved any green bottle of beer and glossy red wallpaper.
Ford told the city to drop dead.

Sylvia Plath was molten ore pouring from the hot pot
sizzling with pods and smashed heads of prawns.

Nixon was still a hand waving from a chopper door—
the war would burn on for a while—

rice paddies would swallow bodies
Vietnamese American soy and mayonnaise.

But—at Tung Lai Shun we learned that the heat
of the tongue could roll images in hot oil along strange circuits

so motion and emotion were more than sense and memory,

just as now I'm in the flow of neuro ice and synaptic glass seeing the river:
those shards, splinters, crystal chandeliers that light up Jersey before dusk.

When we left the place we wobbled down two floors of stairs into
the night-street flow—midwinter blast blowing from the East River.

ODE TO THE DOUDUK

It's not the wind I hear driving south

through the Catskills—it's just bad news from the radio

and then a hailstorm morphs into sunlight

—look up and there's—
an archipelago of starlings trailing some clouds.

But how does the wind come through you—
primordial hollow—unflattened double reed—

so even now when bad news comes with the evening report,
I can press a button on the dashboard and hear your breath implode

the way wind blows through the slit windows of a church in Dilijan,

then a space in my head fills with a sound that rises from red clay dust roads
and slides through your raspy apricot wood.

Hiss of tires, wet tarmac, stray white lines,
night coming like wet dissolve to pixilation—

Praise to the glottal stop of every hoarse whisper, every sodden tree
that speaks through your hollow carved wood—

so we can hear the air flow over starlings rising and dipping
        as the trees fade in sun-glaze

so we can hear the bad news kiss the wind through your reed—

WAITING FOR A NUMBER

Words appeared as the soft purring of a cat, crow screeching,
end of a hymn, cicadas in trees—spilling in the white
noise of my head—Da Nang Mekong Saigon Nam.

I walked suburban streets to school, hi-fi blasting "Somebody to Love,"
coach meting out orders, my playbook of fakes and jives,
my head swelling in the helmet. Over sweet cocktails with my beloved

under the yellowing gingkoes of 64th off Lex, for a moment I felt
grown up, and then the air in my head was orange chemical Dow
and DuPont, the juke box blasting "Light My Fire"—and where were we?

Staring at the image: pistol to the head, a boy I once knew
on the white-lined field was bagged
and flown back in the dioxin haze of morning.

In the mangrove of my head chopping sounds
under the covers, rice paddies—floating mirrors with unidentified
objects. There were Catholics in Saigon and Catholics on my street;

what about Laos? What about Cambodia?
American questions spilling in sunlight on white
shutters, and I'm home on plush carpet waiting for a number.

SUMMER ODE

Today it's gray sky green rain Russian
sage, mauve iris, lavender spiderwort—
what a garden to look out at while I read

Mandelstam's poems of 1928—like reading
the wings of a viceroy on a blue stone.
Then—you called from way over there,
and what happiness filled me up—

and then airwaves came with the news
that thugs had deepened their grip on the country.
Light always shifts before a hurricane.

Remember the black velvet night of the year
when a poet was arrested for doing his work—
his work!—elliptical waterfall of the word.

Every reader can smell the rotting corpse;
every reader can tell when her nation is cast
under a canopy of collapsing trees.

Every reader has a soul that moves like water
under rock; you can't miss the fake hair
of the lubricious lizard as he crawls out of darkness.

For now, *beloved nation* is a phrase hanging
from a live wire. Every reader checks
her passport for facts and truth.

YELLOW LILIES

Looking up—a galaxy is
any star skidding into black.

A black hole is my love. Who knows what's
in the next cushion of air.

What if a hole is just a Greek urn
or Serra's paint-stick spiral?

It's past midsummer and specks
of light are wings of giant birds;

I'll hang my torn soul on that,

take the flash of a star,
the white line of a plane,

hear the ocean sound of words,
hum-blaring horn of wind.

When I wake in gray light:
black rocks, cardinals,

yellow lilies, cumulonimbus.
The grass is drying on me.

A deer's eyes
burn through the pines.

OUTSIDE ARSHILE GORKY'S STUDIO

Buying organic honey and a slab
of blue at the open market—Union Square late day—

look up to see that #36 is covered over by a storefront
selling high-tech stuff, and a light drizzle

coats my head and through the streetlights
I see a church down the block

that jogs me to the big lake and the Armenian church
your mother used to take you to (it's still in Turkey)

where I took some cell phone snaps of the carved
walls as the morning sun like Phaëthon's chariot

lit up the Madonna and Child on the east facade that you worked
over so many times till your brush was down to nothing.

The '29 Crash, bread lines, bullet holes in glass doors.
Why stretch canvasses in the daylight of bad times?

Your friends said you scrubbed your studio floor
with Lysol till it blanched; canvasses raw, scraped, linen.

Wasn't it Hegel who said beauty was
an expression of some sort of freedom?

All roads led to Union Square. Nightmares scoured
by day, turpentine evaporating by night.

REVENANT LOVE

We always woke early under
the half-hammered beams

through which the sky
came and some sounds

of people cheering or
killing each other on another street.

And remember
when we talked into the

early morning before
music came on the only

station we could get
clear at that hour—

sometimes Rachmaninoff
sometimes unknown blues

sometimes an ad for a
foreign car.

Here's a shot of arak

to what was truest about us;
to the way wind comes

through the rafters
and half-wired walls.

I still love watching the lights
go on in the houses down the street.

WATCHING THE TULIPS DIE

You won't go. Deepening
to crimson, fading green stems
sucking up the water of the glass vase,

peeling sides of your petals
vibrating with powdery
anther—speckling the leaves.

Feathered flame, oracular
lover of invisible moons
and white nights,

swollen goblets, Corinthian
whorls of dark spaces
where cochineal birds—still fly.

All morning I stare into your
yellow anthers as they catch the light
through the window.

It's just Dutch madness
craved through plague and fire.
O variation on *T. armena*,

black-streaked red petals
brighter to me than Jan van Huysum's
transcendent illusions on great tables.

Only now—can I see
your elongated necks
on Armenian tiles—

the red underglaze—
fire leaping
from bronze rocks.

PURPLE IRISES

Mouths of the lagoons of Ha Long harbor

swallowing the purple meridians with your yellow clitoral brush.

Outside, the virus snakes like wind through a rainbow of birds—

pathogen—meaning *suffering passion* (Greek)—

path of wind blowing over the saffron of your stigmas—

blowing through the open window—

blowing the electric origin of feeling—

path of the word as it tangles with death

and spring air, with the shock of green flaring from the flank of the pond

from the day that passes like a thousand fronds glistening in the early sun.

I stare at your blades—lipping canyons of invisible whorls.

Out in the deserted streets there's an occasional figure walking in the blue dawn,

then light comes like bearded petals of Maui moonlight.

SHADOW GRID

April 2020

When I came to—crocuses were pushing up
purple in my garden, return of the cooing dove—

and when I got out at Penn Station there were no faces
along the tracks—

wind blew through 32nd Street with a faint whiff of onions
and hair spray

cabs drifted between lanes like bumper cars at Asbury Park

crosswinds; crosstown; the uroboric shape of Columbus Circle.

Etruscan bull's eye. Minoan nude. The cylinder seals of Ur,
stately people on folding stools,

at the Met—in the dark,
the peace, the peace, the peace.

A bird, the stripes of a flag, a floating bridge.

The nation's pleasure myth unspooling
through stadiums and supermarkets.

I see a wavering horizon across borders
from the shanked Palisades below Fort Lee,

air flows through my open window like any day,
innocent coming over the Hudson.

GRASSES OF UNKNOWING

Don't forget the summer of covid
was green with sun in Central New York.

Remember the green was translucent,
yellow-blue, leaf-elm, spruce-needled,

green of Rothko's opaque swaths
green Giotto made with egg yolks on plaster

cataract green of water lilies at Giverny
Gorky green of the gone gardens of Van

translucent green of still-life grapes
sunlit milk pouring out of green majolica

Van Gogh's cypresses in the wind of Arles
blowing into the sage waves of the Rhone—

into the brush of the orchid
in the fronds of Rousseau's jungle

and the green of Mary's ink and wash on board
that woke me before sunrise—

the white wall of my room framing the world
before I gazed on a field of anxious butterflies.

Mind of swaths and emulsions. Grasses of unknowing.
Stay. In the return. Egg yolks on plaster.

HOW MUCH I LOVE YOU

because your shadow walks through the wall

because my heart is a double-beat

because throbbing moves around the room the way
floaters spin across the eye

because the pale green of wet grass
because the confusion of new leaves

because the brushstrokes are blue

because buds of azaleas spread across lawns

because daylight is water

Two

EGGPLANT

I loved the white moon circles
and the purple halos

on a plate as the salt sweat them.

The oil in the pan smoked like bad
days in the Syrian desert—

when a moon stayed all day—

when morning was a purple
elegy for the last friend seen—

when the fog of the riverbank
rose like a holy ghost.

My mother made those white moons sizzle
in some egg wash and salt—

some parsley appeared
from the garden

and summer evenings
came with no memory

but the table with white dishes.

Shining aubergine—black-skinned
beauty, bitter apple.

We used our hands.

QUINCE

Hard-ass, bitter-pucker,
pink-white cheeks of fury,

my grandmother sliced you
on hot Mesopotamian days.

Her name was Athena and she
thought of you as Aphrodite's secret,

because Callimachus wrote his heart out
on your dry skin—

swearing to marry his true love.
We plunked you in a pot

with lye, and when I heard the word
it stuck like moral truth,

and then I learned it was for
alkaline—something I didn't understand.

The hard fruit baked
and oozed some glaze.

It stuck on my tongue

when Gran smeared it
on a hunk of roasted lamb

or mashed it as compote
for the morning.

Autumn road, no map into darkness,
we drove to find you

in black nitrogen and rising sun.
Flesh of flesh

burning, solid, caustic
caritas of lye.

BULGUR

Why did the chipped grains
swirl in butter with onions,

and then become ghostly
when the broth poured?

Umber, straw,
dust of tufa stones—

the mane of Gran's stallion—

husk-protector,
redress to the wind,

hard inversion of rain,

you came from where the stallion
voided over the cliff.

You were a stem downed
by pounding hooves.

When the pot boiled and cooled,

the flying steed of Anatolia
was steam rising to my face.

Ground-broth, silk road,
groats of dead voices,

from snow-ledge marshes
you grew across the borderless land.

Here on the kitchen table, steaming
kernels of light shine on plates.

POMEGRANATE

Persephone ate you
and went to hell.

My grandmother
walked with you under her blouse—

her two daughters
hobbling with her.

Every day one seed
for each of them.

Whatever death road
they walked down

you were: seed-apple,
garnet, cochineal,

spiritus ovum—

spiraling hawk-dive
of the soul—

leather-red skin
for hard times.

Sometimes she looked up
at the moon and saw you.

MATZA

Sometimes when I look up at the moon
I think of Alan Schwartz

in whose kitchen I sat on Passover
(we were the only Christians on the block)—

eating corrugated sheets of bread—
though it didn't feel like bread.

In the evening, the moon's white light
followed me home.

I didn't understand what God
commanded the Jews to do.

At the Formica counter before the Seder
we crunched on the mother of all wafers.

Out of Egypt there was moonlight
over the stillness.

Crisp and sweet to the tongue.
Was this the bread of affliction?

Years later when Alan was shot out
of the sky over the Sinai, I asked the moon:

What was the no-yeast of freedom?

I walked for days to get to the Red Sea,
because Exodus led to Deuteronomy.

Even now when I'm shivering at the water's edge,
the sky no more blue than ash over trees,

the difference between prophecy and law
is the difference between the moon and the sea.

The end of the body is one half of death,
the absence of moonlight—the other.

FIG

The body wasn't meant to be covered
in shame.

Fresh or dry I sucked your seeds
in winter and summer after dinner.

I've no idea why Jesus cursed you
because a drought had done you in.

Your self-pollinating powers averted
every curse, no matter what the text says.

Once I picked a few of you
off a tree outside of Aleppo,

tawny purple skin
fleshy sex sac—

honey—sucked on hard days
by refugees in bad places.

Sunsets came over you,
gauzy pink hanging there

like Fragonard wisps
or gooey dew on perfect mornings,

waiting to be picked for slake
and a sure view of the horizon—

Mission-black, stuck to cellophane,
Kalamata, pulled off a hard string,

I packed you in a knapsack
for my trek into the Syrian desert

scouring for remains of the dead—

Even though I did return,
what I saw was your cursed absence.

At sunset I chewed on you
back under the flag of a torn nation,

walking toward the hotel
dinner clatter in earshot,

I couldn't use your leaf to cover
over anything.

WALNUT

Leonardo used you to make ink.

A friend once gave me
a three-segment for luck.

My mother chopped you to fine
gravel with cinnamon and sugar.

Leonardo's crosshatches
were the wrinkles of your shell.

I followed my mother's hand
across a vague sky on Good Friday

because she made your shaved dust into
morning light,

your female estuaries pulled me in.

Leonardo found the womb inside your shell—
and washed some light into the dark sky.

You left a sheen on my hand.

APRICOT

Lightning hit you
from the orchard cliff

and something
poured into your

pink-orange
in the mud-black.

I lay in your shade
with hands that touched mine

the way light touches air.
Wind blew through our eyes.

We ate you sun-clean

as hawks swooped over us—
labyrinthitis of the sky.

We felt the earth,
sunlight was our blanket,

your juice grazed our tongues
red-tinged skin spilled your seeds.

It could have been St. Elmo
sizzling your branches.

Dozens dropped on us—

sun-fire, stone-pit—
we bit the skin with our nails.

GRAPE LEAVES

We trellised you on fences
and in our heads as old markers of lost places.

We lipped you full of pine nuts,
currants and rice. You, the polymorphic leaf,

libation for the un-chosen,
Jesus and Bacchus in one.

You—who fanned the hermaphroditic flower
in the heat of early summer,

before we blanched you in hot water
softened you to roll and soak.

You were the pale green blank page on which I saw
some style of unthinkable events

working your veins.
You were always tender and soft

like parchment on which
light shifted during long days.

Unilluminated manuscript,
postmarked with scars and blood—

calligraphed by wind and sun
whenever unforeseen events rolled over you.

I want always to taste your sweet
filling, the oil glistening on someone else's lips.

TOMATOES

My mother hovered over the staked
vines, the sweet fuzz of pale green stems.

By August the heavy air leaned on them.
When the sky cracked with lightning

the stakes held the rain
and the fat beefsteaks swelled.

On a chopping board, I ran a serrated
knife across their thin skin for thick slices;

water poured from the pulp and seeds
of the quadrants.

Whatever churned out there in the
news of irradiated rice paddies,

the burning white streets of America,
whatever hurricane was coming up

from the unknown waters, whatever fate
was brewing in the hungry lots across town,

I soaked you up with bread and salt—
nightshade of sun, the Navajo called you.

OKRA

My mother stewed you
with onions and tomatoes

then rice and chicken stock
to simmer for hours

so when I came in from the sandlot
with some bloodied arm or face

your steam was a counterplay.
It took me a while to savor

the slide of your slimy pods
down my throat—

your seeds rolled
the roof of my mouth—

the pods floated like caïques
in the broth.

But I came to see your hieroglyphics
in red clay

because Black women sizzled you up
in the big house

to rebut the theft,
to smuggle in home:

canoes of the Niger—
dug-out tree trunks,

pirogues of the heart
of rushing water—

origin of gumbo:
ok u ru in Igbo—

words on the roof of my mouth—
anagrams in broth.

ZUCCHINI

My grandmother cored them
with a serrated knife

with her hands that had come
through the slaughter—

So many hours I stared at the blotch
marks on her knuckles

her strong fingers around the
long green gourd.

In a glass bowl the stuffing was setting—
chopped lamb, tomato pulp, raw rice, lemon juice,

a sand brew of spices
from the riverbank of her birth.

Can holding on to this image
help me make sense of time?

The temporal waves,
waves smashing and lipping

the pulverized stone; a bird dissolving
into a cloud bank in late day;

the happy and sad steps we walked

along the plaster walls and steel bridges,
the glass facades, highways of glistening money—

objects we caress in dreams
from which we wake to find the hallway dark

the small light at the bottom of the stairs,
the kitchen waiting with a scent

of zucchini, sautéed in olive oil
garlic, oregano,

a waft of last night's red wine—a gulp
of cold water to bring on the day.

Three

NO SIGN

1.
He: Is it night already?

She: No.

He: Did our house fall down?

She: What happened?

He: Is it you?

2.
He: Yes.

She: Why should I believe you?

He: Doesn't geology put us in our place?

*

He: We appeared in the age of fission:
vaporized bodies, ionized dragonflies, shadows printed on stone.

She: Japanese cities burned in my dreams.
        I saw the newsreels in class
decades later—

He: We're back here on the Palisades cliffs—staring at Manhattan—
        remember when the Sauternes was liquid gold?

3.
She: In the beginning there were alpha particles and gamma rays.

We always see daylight through the kitchen window near dusk
We can't forget how dusk turns the hydrangea deep blue.

We can't forget the glowing dioxin sun—the no-gaze,
morning bright blue agent-orange sky—even now—after all.

4.
He: Godard called *Hiroshima mon amour* Faulkner plus Stravinsky—

She: Remember: at the Angelika—September smell of light rain
warm sidewalks shop awnings   late summer—

He: The noren curtains opened, the noren curtains closed.

We stared at kanji, birds, sketches of roofs, a tree

the lovers walked through the curtains either way

time shifted like breeze through eye sockets

She: They said goodbye and the noren curtains opened
and   the past was a   burning city
seen in silence, just images on screens.

Lui: What did Hiroshima mean to you?

Elle: The end of the war, fear and terror that it could happen to us,
then indifference—astonishment that they dare do it—
then it became an unknown fear—

5.
She: We're standing—

on an underground channel of molten rock
that fed volcanic eruptions 200 million years ago.

Earth = axis = spinning = two selves—swerve—possibility

He: Take Pan, all day we've played around with him.

She: Here we are—lying on Gaea.

He: Top of a volcano—molten basalt cooled and hardened

   we're on the sill still, and rock is never still—

She: The sill's eastern edge = Palisades cliffs, one version of home.

6.
He: Unified land mass—Pangea—Earth as whole—

She: Pan and Gaea = bridging self with other.

7.
He: Remember the blizzard of letters—
commas, question marks, dashes, words cut in half
on the subway walls at 4th—after we talked out the movie

you said—one view of the post-war:
a burger and a shake, a jukebox and a neon rainbow on the wall.

51

8.
He: If you said it was molten rock, I believed you.
If you said the molten rock was once underground

and created volcanic eruptions 200 million years ago,
I believed you.

If you said the eruptions covered 4 million square miles with
basalt lava, I didn't flinch.

And if the lava blasted gales of carbon dioxide and sulfur into the atmosphere,
I got the general idea.

I got the general idea that there were long volcanic winters after and after—

like sci-fi on a screen in a movie house at the beginning of time
when the reception was perfect.

She: Listen to Gaea: "We broke apart—200 million years ago—end of Triassic—

magma rose from deeper in the earth

intruded into the sandstones and shales, then the molten rock spread, cooled,
    hardened,
then—I was a sill overlaying softer rock—and the softer rock eroded."

9.
He: The look of ionized skin of the two lovers in bed
—the caressing, the trick of the camera

—irradiated light: those oboes and violins—
and the skeletal flutes—same as *Night and Fog*—

Lui: You saw nothing.
Elle: I saw everything.

Elle: How could I have not seen it?
Lui: You saw nothing in Hiroshima.

10.
She: Can you imagine the perfect eruptions until the clouds dissolved—
and the ocean became acidic like a white-out gale and

the atmosphere heated up until most of life on Earth
was impossible?

Did you get the picture of Triassic extinction? Not many
creatures survived but giant lizards came to be the shape and form

we think of now when we take in this idea—even as the big screen breaks
down into a blank stare.

11.
He: Under the tulip trees in June

in the high grass of the Palisades

the sunlit bands across our bodies—

lying under the cicada-pulsating,
tree-rattling, shaking green-blur

cicatrix of leaves dissolving into
caterpillars—chartreuse fur

into the violet flares of the sky—
sounds of the oboes of Brahms,

we loved the hovering iridescent

dragonflies, a luna's green-wing
glow—the river water spilling

on the high grass
translucent moss on our backs.

12.
He: If you insist that the next 136 million years were dominated by the
giant reptiles until an asteroid struck the place we now call Mexico

and the explosion ended the era of the lizards,
I can try to take that in—with or without the screen—

the imagination is limited even if we deny it.

13.
He: What Elle saw in the Hiroshima Peace Museum—what of it?

She: The illusion is also real—

what else can a tourist do but weep—
the burnt children in stupor like puppets—

city of ash and rubble, scorched metal.

He: Remember—Elle said: *I saw the newsreels on the second day*
the emphatic sensuality of her diction:
deuxième jour, troisième jour, quinzième jour—

you were pulled in by it.

She: I still love her.

14.
He: Am I still stuck to you

like volcanic wetness,
like paint on canvass

pours, stick-wipes, splatters

She: I to you—in absence that kisses me—
thinned out on floors and boards,
like lava on flax—the glue of hands—

He: Craving for—sand, yolks, linseed oil—
soak the pulp as the Egyptians did—

15.
He: In the film it went like this:

Lui: You made it all up

Elle: None of it

On the fifteenth day Hiroshima was covered with cornflowers and gladiolas,
morning glories and daylilies—a strange fertility emerged

Lui: You made it all up

Elle: Just as the illusion exists in love—
*   Those in the wombs of the women—*

Then Resnais' cut from deformed hands to her glistening fingers on his
    chest—

Lui: Nothing. You know nothing—

16.
She: inert gases—then millions of years for oxygen to flow into it—

think of light as diffuse gamma rays spreading on the body of air—

He: Pan's idea of swamps coming into anthracite—
    fossilized leaf debris—

She: Gaea would say: detritus is a portrait of us.

17.
He: American implosion: Conservative need to
    deny history

She: Go back to Vietnam; the nation should have learned from it.

18.
He: I was your scent-carrier,

your rose-burning sun

we lived between hard rocks and clouds—

sussurring leaves licked us
crepuscular light loved us.

fading light over the Cloisters

everything dissolving into everything,
the bridge lights go on,

then the beyond: always implied by
the absence hanging over the cliffs.

19.
She: There was Dien Bien Phu—essential—
a ghost of grainy footage on some old reel

on which French soldiers slid down hillsides
like ants in glue—

the gray pixilated dissolve of 1954—the reality pill
down the hatch with no water—

He: refusal to learn from history.

She: Later—after Tet:

"We heard small Buddhist chimes ringing for peace in Hoa Bien."

Hanoi Nagasaki Saigon Hiroshima
Keep saying it—it will sink in.

2019—here—again—no light at end of the tunnel

no sign—

20.
She: For hundreds of millions of years orogenic forces crushed
these stones—until they became mountains—that's Gaea's message:

millennia of abrasion by the ocean
decapitated headlands and broken rock.

He: We're standing on bloated eons of cliff crevice—

She: Rocks are time—(tell that to the fundamentalists)
                    feel them in your bones
like a coal seam,
              the origin of the Hudson flowing down there

leaf debris
          pre-Cambrian stone
inscriptions beneath our feet.

21.
He: Who was there in the defoliated jungle,
the burning water spreading over bodies—

fuck // that was where Gaea and Pan
were supposed to hold hands

and walk across the DMZ ('68 Paris talks derailed)

that was the vision / wiped out /
by Nixon's scheme—for election = more

than a million dead.

She: Remember I loved you in the DMZ,
north and south, either/or

I loved you there—

22.
She: Forget about Gaea's offspring for now—

a creation myth is one way to understand
what the imagination reaches for—

He: We're here // facing something

we can't imagine—

23.
He: From the riverbank
it looked like a broken tower,

fog swallowing the vaults

light spilling out of clouds—

I saw cochineal birds

falling through bare steel, gray metallic
silver cables, nuts and bolts

—call it the functional sublime—blaring sheen

steel saddles holding giant barrel-cables

all night the humming in my head,

the burning tires going north to New England—

24.
He: As the fog blew off the bridge,

half crocked—
we walked the deco gun-metal

following some parabolic arc of steel—

we ran all night under the fuselage-tubes vibrating over us—

who knew then they were made of spun wires,
galvanized steel, 107,000 miles of it—enough to wrap
the globe 4 times—halfway to the moon (no metaphor)—

434 wires making up a strand of 3 inches—

anchorages tied the towers to the Palisades—
cut 45 feet down in the rock of the riverbed—

16 towers of steel floated on barges
June '28—Herbert Hoover's face

was bright; the moon passed between
Earth and the sun. The river was clear.

We sat at the edge looking down at the dark water.

25.
She: Between Can Tho and Saigon

*there were men in deep depression // manic nightmares
howling in mildew sheets.*

Saigon was a final reel of On the Beach, *a desolate city*
whose long avenues held nothing but refuse, windblown papers,
small piles of human excrement, spent firecracker casings of the Lunar New Year.

26.
He: After work, after sun-fade—

trucks and cars amped to Jersey and west—

the cables—joining dreamers—
stringer-lights flashing our faces.

We were lit up in t-shirts and jeans,
the West Side lighting the river,

the galvanized wires like magnetic fingertips
and plucks, guitar reverb distortion

overdrive—space between notes

a pistol shot, a siren.
Sometimes the whole bridge was a VST plug-in

amped in sync with untamable variations—(like Hendrix)
—flattened out cable distortion.

All night we bounced through falsetto plug-ins.

27.
She: translucent blur, shell fragment // white sparks smoke drift

running tremor in the earth—

28.
She: Sometimes we were intimate, erotic, heat-waved
when the worst things were happening outside
in the big ugly world—our glass window on the Hudson
was a strange camera lens fading out the violence—
then we came and came to and got back out there.

29.
He: What caused the K-T mass extinction?

She: Darwin was aware of the discontinuity at the end of the Cretaceous—

He: Why is ocean acidification so dangerous?

She: "It changes the microbial communities"

toxic algae, falling ocean pH—CO_2—
impact of human greed = carbon fossil fuel fire—

He: You saw Paradise, California on fire; you saw Java and Sumatra
crash in the seismic sea—

read the sign—

She: Remember what Lucretius said:
"unless inclined to swerve all things would fall."

30.
She: Why are we hanging from this cliff
why these fragments—why these word-chips like mica—
like scree coming down now on us as we //

He: Look at the Hudson in the purple dusk,
when we can barely see the water, it's at fullest surge

—here and now—
spraying onto the rocks, driving
our gaze inward and out in one breath.

31.
He: No dream: the exit ramp at 175—we got
off the A-Train—blown away—under the silver sky

of the towers—the beacon lights sliding down
the cables—electric mist on my arms—

high-pass hum, no filter—

voltage of the insomniac walkway into the black—

distorted wave forms—it's what I'm after—
non-linear currents—

a revenant hand on the keyboard
just valve over-drive, a cathode unstrung—

light-spots   shadow-tips   sundial traces—
big zoom purple fringing everywhere—

(magenta ghosts you called them)

under the cloudy stars—the wind spray
drench of evening brought me back to you—

running through a wall of sound
a vacuum tube—

strung out on a geodesic curve.

32.
Lui: Nothing, you know nothing

Elle: Food became an object of fear

Lui: You don't know what it is to forget

Elle: No, you are not endowed with memory

Lui: Like you I longed for a memory beyond consolation

Elle: Against the horror of no longer understanding

Lui: A memory of shadows and stone

Elle: I have struggled not to forget

33.
She: And now. The inconceivable,
      with Trump everything's a moving target—
including the Earth—

He: Trump signing Bibles after a tornado in Alabama—

She: the price of losing reality.

34.
He: After we split—I lived for

days under the sunsets of Zaum
sky above—bridge below.

If the shortest route between ends
is a single point where light meets—

then purple fringing along the river
was my site line and I lived in it for a while

watching the lights of the Triboro
and flashing reds of the airport—

headlights of cars going west—

the black ribbon of route 80 vanishing from the bridge lights
to the Water Gap—

breathing the vibrato air
fretboard cables—trusses, plate girders—wires—

35.
She: Remember the shadow cast by the sun, axial spin of Earth—

time // stone // self = postmodern homo sapiens—

remember the heat of the pre-Cambrian sun   remember Pangaea.

36.
He: When will the sun bloat into a red giant—after the oceans are boiled away
and the Earth is bleached—

She: But now Sauternes light coming down over the Palisades

Solid to liquid to gas—H_2O—to CO_2—

tree as life—

Pan meeting Gaea.

37.
He: Remember—the air was still, trees motionless, the sky touched my chest—
here at the rocks on the river edge I came to feel:

—how does the soul speak?

Does it come out of the blue or out of some recondite preparation—
unknown to us in day?

38.
She: I was under the illusion that I will never forget Hiroshima.

He: The flash was a giant yellow light—*bokuzuki* were useless
the houses in the neighborhood evaporated—

She: The illusion is so perfect that the tourists cry.

He: What else can a tourist do?

39.
She: We're heating up—biotic attrition is just a euphemism

a quarter of all species heading into the black hole—

He: what about the phyla of books, music, art, zigzag of buildings-to-god
    going in the slow flash—

40.
She: "Nothing can be brought back into nothingness nor be created
                              out of naught" (Lucretius)

He: "Who teaches the soul?" (Juan de la Cruz)—

how the daemon comes and goes not like a bolt
but like the breeze of a curtain opening.

66

41.
He: As for radioactive dating of rock; re-think mile-stones = milestones—
                    life in hand—

bronze light of late day off the river—
the momentary sheen—

She: Signifying something between souls.
Love remains as the seam and the rock.

Dusk turns the hydrangeas deep blue.

42.
He: I rowed under the sunlit towers,

light pouring down on the concrete vaults

magenta birds diving into the sun-bubbling waves—

tugs and barges fading into gold haze.

43.
She: Think of Monet painting blind the emptiness of blue;
top of the skull rises into the smoke from distant Queens

into the lily pond of the sky,
smooth brush of horizon.

Van Gogh said absolute black does not exist—
keep in mind—his joy—in the purple shadow moving over us

as the dark comes—just as now the black silhouettes of Shadow
Man are visible in the night facades—

44.
He: I know beneath this hull is rift and subduction
underwater jazz and terror—as if Sun Ra and Chopin embraced
beneath a surface they didn't understand—

She: —remember: light spills as dark comes—chalk floats off the silhouettes.

45.
Lui: *You saw nothing.*
Elle: *I saw everything.*

Lui: *What did it mean to you?*

The curtains are always moving—
light turns the hydrangea deep blue.

Four

STALLED IN TRAFFIC

under the overpass of the Cross Bronx,
the headlights flash on broken

concrete between cars and exit ramp and some
undefined hunk of metal rising out of broken glass

and the disconnected passage that got us to Manhattan
comes to me like a collage of cities cut off the map.

All I know is my father left Constantinople
in 1922, on a train in the dark snaking into Thrace

and his mother's hand became a trace of history,
a U-turn of collapsing latitudes

as the tracks disappeared into Greece.
By the time they arrived in Vienna
the Prater was hypnotic—a shattered wheel

of glass through which to see the
Bosphorus sludge and iridescent
petrol from the docks where the caïques

wharfed and the mussel shells poured
like black gems. In the Armenian cemetery
of Scutari my grandfather stone-rubbed some

names—the shapes of flying dragons
my father passed to me.

71

HEAD OF ANAHIT/BRITISH MUSEUM

I.

You said anyone could walk in
with a pack of explosives as we passed through
the crowds of tourists and school kids—

under the glass-grid ceiling lit with sun.

I was saying: *She's our earth, our body, our sex,*
as we drifted down the halls of statues and colonnades
and hunks of facades of Greek temples until we found

Room 22 *The Hellenistic World* where a face
in a glass box on the wall stared back at us.

Head from a bronze cult statue
Of Anahita, a local goddess
In the guise of Aphrodite (200-100 BC)

The text hung there in space: *Found in Satala in NE Asia Minor*
(Armenia Minor)

a left hand holding drapery was found with the head //

and out of some bad Comedy Central joke,
my iPhone buzzed with a flash news update
about ISIS or ISIL, or whatever they called themselves this week—

Temple of Baalshamin at Palmyra—blown-up—
the phrase re-circled—*blown up—*

2.

and my head was back in the white van with the *60 Minutes* crew,
winding through the buttes and roadside gullies of the Syrian desert,
to the Armenian memorial in Der Zor,

before going to Palmyra, where I sat under
50-foot Corinthian columns—
the corners chipped by wind and sand

in late May when it hit 110 °F at noon
and the sun melting the plastic rim of my cell phone—
as our driver appeared out of nowhere with stacks

of za'atar bread and Diet Cokes—
we found some shade under a portico
as the visionary pillars disappeared into blue sky.

3.

Outside students were buzzing through the gates
of UCL and the brown brick of Bloomsbury was lit up
with sun after rain—

Inside the *Wunderkammer* of Hans Sloane
stuffed with the stolen stuff from the Middle East—

("What is the Middle East," my Turkish publisher
asked an audience at NYU—
"Istanbul, Jerusalem, Mumbai, Srinagar?")

you kept asking: "What is year zero to us?
Didn't our war destroy some temples and museums?"

I called the curator on the phone at the info desk
to leave my complaint on the message machine
about the signage:

"Zatala wasn't *Armenia Minor / NE Asia Minor*—
it was central Armenia Anatolia—make correction."

4.
What questions were we asking,
staring at the misinformation on the wall
and the beautiful Armenian head of Anahit?

Why was I back in Der Zor at the chapel
digging Armenian bones out of the baked ground—
scratching the marrow and dried mildew?

5.
In the age of throat slitting on Twitter,
the imperial shock and awe of the burning Tigris—
the lynching of Saddam on the internet,
vanishing tomb of Jonah—

Who owns the fetishized objects . . . whose museum?

6.
I'm gazing at the head of Anahit—Armenian
goddess of fertility and love—
(no more local than the Brooklyn Bridge)

staring at the green and red paint still speckled on her bronze head.
I love her serpentine upper lip, her eyes of black space—

I stare into the screw hole in her neck
the two curlicues of hair on her forehead
her august throat, her dense acanthine hair.

COMING TO ISTANBUL

Follow the gaze of Athena
down a cistern where water glows.

Follow silver snakes along Marmara
and Golden Horn.

Walk over the black plaque for Hrant Dink
smack in the street in Shishli.

Follow the ferry-waves to Üsküdar—
where your father was born,

where your uncle returned
incognito from prison—

Drink the split bourbon voice of Ray Charles
in the café in Taxsim

under the red flags of star and moon
guns to the head, wild prayer—

streets banging with pots and pans—
rage at the dictator.

Walk by in oblivion and terror
an American, an Armenian, black shirt

under the olive-trellised restaurant
hotel rooftop light-rinsed Bosphorus

hot raki fumes in the throat
under the wind-umbrellas

and boutique-class facades of Beyoglu
galleries of blue mosaics, magenta carpets—

the Ottoman historian pours you
tahn and wine into the sunset.

Follow the lights on the bridge
into the chandelier of the sky

trompe l'oeil of Gray Wolves
voices of Turkish friends in the stone.

Follow ghost signs midnight cab
smashed café windows

night-sea journey of beloveds
Byzantine dirt smoke roads

past Tobacco Regie and sultana crates—
Haydarpasha of Armenian-soul death hour.

Lost family come greet me in your city.

LEAVING THE BIG CITY

So afterward I sat by the Bosphorus blue water and many dazzling

shapes smoothed the air; somehow the mind grew still as

a shadow passed through and the shore was occluded by small boats
                                                 and overhanging roofs.

Out of nothing—sounds of the daily world broke through and came

as an affront to what was lost. Rushing traffic sounds died in my head.

Tourists moved through streets and the smoke of grilling meats and balm of spices.

Once my father was a reflection on a wall, and time collapsed for the time of listening

to what couldn't be imagined and the sound of that elusive boy among

other boys who found passage out on ships and trains, who stuffed themselves

into a crease the way a sock is folded into itself and stuffed inside a satchel

and the satchel moved across latitudes with the clarity of shadows.

WALKING THE RUINED CITY
Turkish/Armenian border

I.

Driving past ravines gouged by ice—sheep dissolve into limestone,
the air darkens like pumice, and then rain comes and wipes

the dirt off the windshield, and we head for the ridges
where the magpies blur and lead me into the stone

2.

and into the echo of voices across the canyon and all
of a sudden—the oblivion ha-ha of foundation walls,

the flow of vines and pomegranates, and in a flint of sun: wings of eagles.
Here—I feel emptiness—deserted in the cut ravines and marsh grass.

I'm sorry about our mixed signals. I wish you
were here now where cows walk in and out of the main cathedral,

their faces aplomb in the light shafting down the big gouges
in the walls. Here the day is eternal, the lingo of dates more alive

3.

than the ecstasy of saints. "Why does the sight of stone
soothe the ear?" Bonnefoy asked; I'd rather say the stones are sexy,

like your open mouth in the sun-splatted morning.
I'm fine in this yellow light curdling the thick grass blowing

78

4.

where the Mongol walls rise with their restorations and pocked
turrets full of diamond shapes and spinning crosses,

and there—where they slant to rubble—there was Tamerlane
and Alp Arslan. Walking the ruins of Ani at the Turkish border,

I can see Armenia clear as grass through the wire
fence on the other side of the river—you would

5.

agree—in this place one lives in the geo. I pass the ticket guard
who asks for money: money which is the face of the conquering

army, money which is the pickax of the disappeared; money which
disappears in the aubergine rain and the magenta bugs of the Armenian marshes.

I nudge Rachel: "Tell the guards, '*You* should pay us,'"
and she repeats it in Turkish, and the burly guy in the ticket booth

stares, takes our money—hands us an eight-lira
tam billet—a beautiful tourist ticket in royal blue which I caress in my hand

like money. Thinking of your hand-caress.

6.

Over cracked stones and gouged grass, I can see the Arkhurian River
where the canyon makes a rough circle around the city—and the light flashes

off the caves in the ravine walls on the Armenian side of the border.
I'm thinking of you waking to Sonny Rollins and the train moving under the bridge.

Here the bridge is gone and a broken wall crumbles into the river,
the Armenian palace circa 975 still has shaped walls on the ramparts,

7.
but the wind off the river takes me by the hand and I stare
at the big cathedral, the one designed by Trdat, and the walls—big hewn

tufa stones: red, terra-cotta, black, cocoa, puce, coral charcoal, chocolate, tan.
Here comes the scree of Saint Gregory, the lamentations of Nareg,

the raucous grass of the smashed-up roof where the magpies roost and shit;
the tiles dissolve in acid rain and radio waves coming down from Georgia—

sounds of douduks, guitars, sax and trumpet, church organ and goat brays.
The word Armenia appears nowhere on any sign or wall—outlawed by the state.

8.
Black holes of caves suck me in like a sour pucker of the dried-up days of 1920.
The wind comes in from the Black Sea; the silence is a monk's breath;

the rain comes and goes; who drank from the chalice here,
were the frescos Chalcedonian?

9.
Why do I feel that here—the body is nothing—*chee-ga, rien, nada.*
Why do pulverized stones give my soles buoyancy?

I've got ghosts in my pockets. My jeans are full of briars,
my Yankees hat blew into the canyon. The arches of the cathedral

stood up under earthquakes and fires because they were hollow—
a small piece of genius. The Pakratuni Kings built it circa 1001

along the Silk Road to Afghanistan and China.
Didn't the forgiving stone love those masons?

Didn't we press into each other in the dead of night—
our bones wired to the sounds of morning—

10.
Out of lava, steam, magma, the pressure of matter on nothing—
all day I grazed the ash beds and fossil shells—the accumulation of life

on the planet, the planet in a compressed block of honed stone—
the honed stone hoisted up to the basilica ceilings and the conical domes

looking out at a valley of caves and yellow flowers.

11.
Mandelstam who loved Yerevan's baked scroll,
Bonnefoy who was haunted by Armenia's churches—

come graze on the stone of free verse: aubade of buttresses,
ghazal of barreled vaults, terza rima of blind arcades, villanelle of niches,

sonnet of squinches, pantoum of pointed arches, sestina of cylinders.
O piers of the radiating arches of Holy Redeemer—wall ribs and colonettes,

O the vigilant powers that keep changing color in the rain.
Who envisioned the cruciform dome plan? Who made the barrel

vaults and pointed arches? How is the traffic on the bridge
out of Brooklyn now? Is there one river that winds around the world?

(It was your question.) Here, graffiti wipes out the Armenian words.

12.

In the Honents Church with its sliced-off roof,
its halos of saints, hands of apostles under white-washed walls,

I was staring at the gold light streaming in
when my friend from Istanbul leading a group of tourists

stared at me in shock. "You've come! Come after all—
after all—after the broken plans and rebooked flights."

We sat on the ruined ledge of the smashed altar with lit candles,
inhaling ashy frankincense as the French women began singing

Devormayah (Lord Have Mercy), and their wavering voices flew
up the ocular hole where the hawks swoop.

13.
O Joan of Arc, Antigone, Phaedra. O birds of Chalcedon—shit
on the heads of parishioners, eat the seeds out of the eyes of the faithful.

14.
What do Turkish schoolkids think when they come here on class trips?

15.
I'm full of apricots and tea and honeycomb. I'm searching for bread.

Are you on the bridge now? Here the light is coming

over the border from Armenia. I'm off the grid for a while.

"Tung Lai Shun": for Bruce Smith.
"Outside Arshile Gorky's Studio": for Atom Egoyan.
"Watching the Tulips Die": for Armen Marsoobian.
"Quince": for Bob Barsamian.
"Bulgur": for Karen Derderian.
"Pomegranate": for Lynn Derderian.
"Matza": for Wendy Ranan.
"Apricot": for Mary Behrens.
"Grape Leaves": for Alice Thomasson.
"Zucchini": for Robert Garland.
"Stalled in Traffic": for Aram Arkun.
"Head of Anahit/British Museum": for Donna-Lee Frieze and
    Michael Coyle.
"Coming to Istanbul": for Taner Akçam.
"Leaving the Big City": for Ragip Zarakolu.

"No Sign": Italicized lines are from the film *Hiroshima mon amour* (1959), script by Marguerite Duras and Alain Resnais. The following sources were useful in writing parts of the following sections:

Sections 19, 25, and 28: Michael Herr, *Dispatches* (1977)
Sections 20 and 37: Paul Pinet, *Shadowed by Deep Time* (2017)
Section 30: Lucretius, *The Nature of Things*, trans. A. E. Stallings (2015)
Sections 30, 40, and 42: Elizabeth Kolbert, *The Sixth Extinction* (2014)
Section 39: John Hersey, *Hiroshima* (1946)